CHRISTMAS CAROLS
with a Classical Flair

15 FAVORITES ARRANGED BY PHILLIP KEVEREN

— PIANO LEVEL —
INTERMEDIATE/LATE INTERMEDIATE

ISBN 978-1-5400-5413-5

HAL•LEONARD®

Visit Hal Leonard Online at
www.halleonard.com

Visit Phillip at
www.phillipkeveren.com

Contact us:
Hal Leonard
7777 West Bluemound Road
Milwaukee, WI 53213
Email: info@halleonard.com

In Europe, contact:
Hal Leonard Europe Limited
42 Wigmore Street
Marylebone, London, W1U 2RN
Email: info@halleonardeurope.comm

In Australia contact:
Hal Leonard Australia Pty. Ltd.
4 Lentara Court
Cheltenham, Victoria, 3192 Australia
Email: info@halleonard.com.au

PREFACE

I am a Christmas music aficionado. I own countless holiday CDs and print music books. I look forward to hearing new recordings that come out each season, never tiring of yet another rendition of the carol canon. It's a good thing I love this music, because – as an arranger and orchestrator – I end up working on Christmas arrangements year-round. In the piano publishing world, my manuscripts need to be turned in by at least April or May. Christmas always seems to be just around the corner!

Bringing beloved carols together with the "classical" style is a pleasure, and a natural fit. Musical inspiration comes from Bach, Mozart, Fauré, Vaughan Williams, and beyond. In the end, I am more interested in unified piano settings than stylistic purity.

Merry Christmas,

Phillip Keveren

BIOGRAPHY

Phillip Keveren, a multi-talented keyboard artist and composer, has composed original works in a variety of genres from piano solo to symphonic orchestra. Mr. Keveren gives frequent concerts and workshops for teachers and their students in the United States, Canada, Europe, and Asia. He holds a B.M. in composition from California State University Northridge and a M.M. in composition from the University of Southern California.

CONTENTS

4 ANGELS FROM THE REALMS OF GLORY

7 ANGELS WE HAVE HEARD ON HIGH

10 COVENTRY CAROL

12 DING DONG! MERRILY ON HIGH!

16 GOD REST YE MERRY, GENTLEMEN

19 THE HURON CAROL
(’TWAS IN THE MOON OF WINTERTIME)

22 IN THE BLEAK MIDWINTER

24 IT CAME UPON THE MIDNIGHT CLEAR

27 JOY TO THE WORLD

30 LET ALL MORTAL FLESH KEEP SILENCE

32 O COME, ALL YE FAITHFUL

38 O HOLY NIGHT

35 SILENT NIGHT

42 STILL, STILL, STILL

44 WE THREE KINGS OF ORIENT ARE

ANGELS FROM THE REALMS OF GLORY

Words by JAMES MONTGOMERY
Music by HENRY T. SMART
Arranged by Phillip Keveren

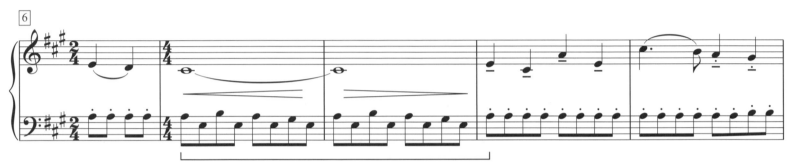

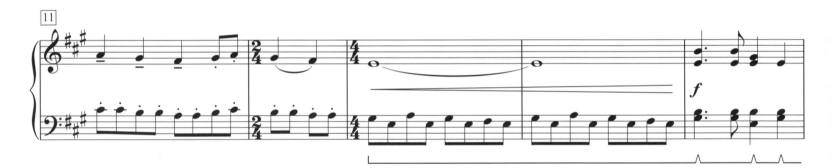

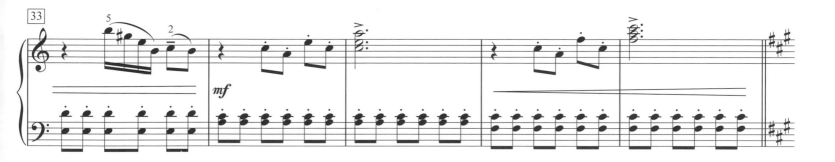

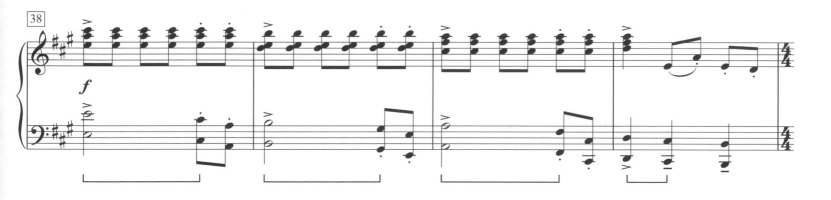

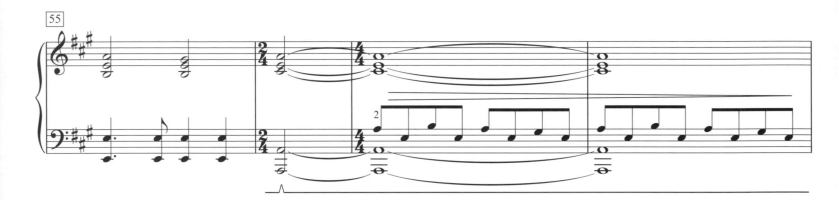

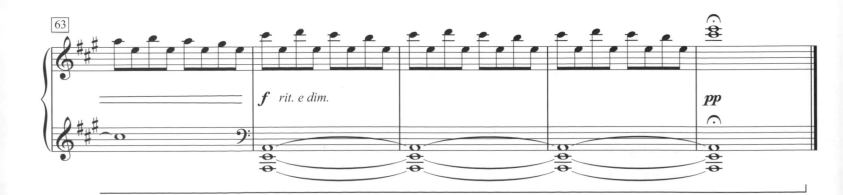

ANGELS WE HAVE HEARD ON HIGH

Traditional French Carol
Translated by JAMES CHADWICK
Arranged by Phillip Keveren

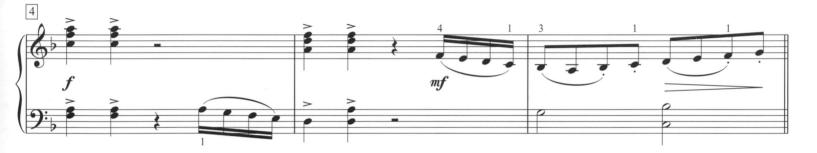

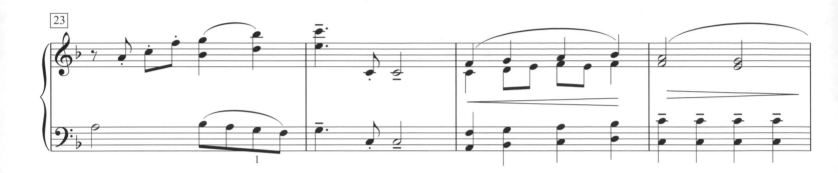

COVENTRY CAROL

Words by ROBERT CROO
Traditional English Melody
Arranged by Phillip Keveren

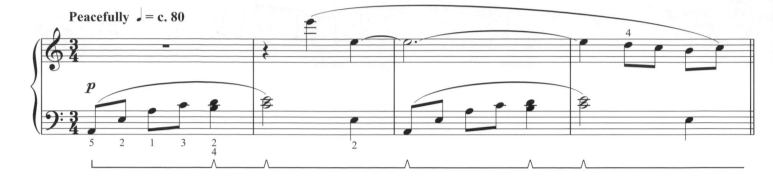

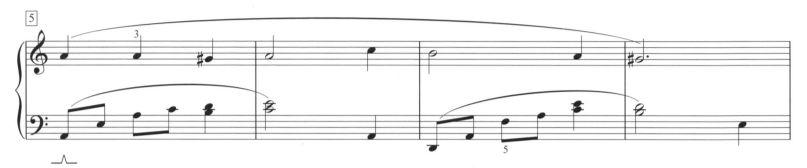

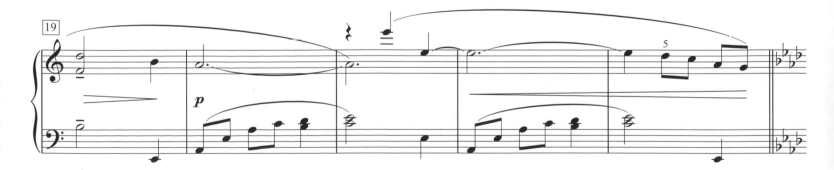

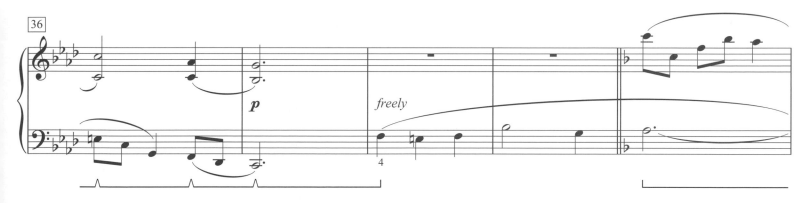

DING DONG! MERRILY ON HIGH!

French Carol
Arranged by Phillip Keveren

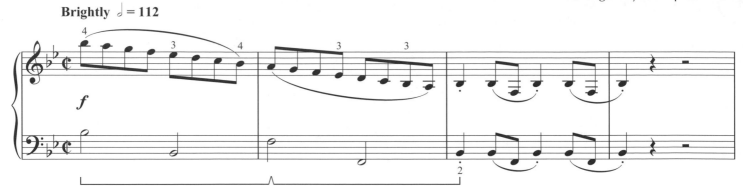

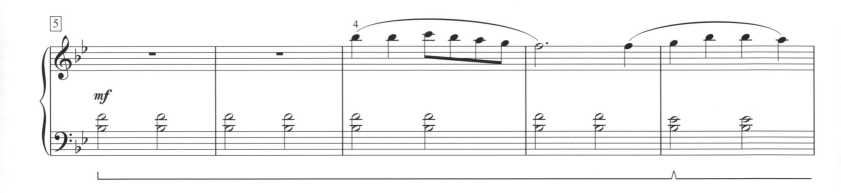

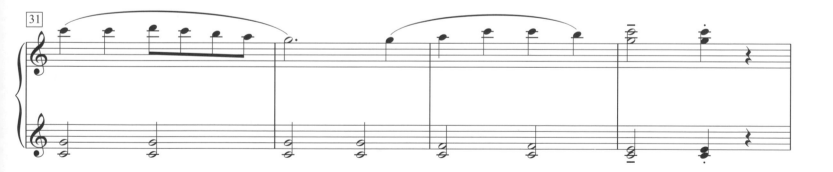

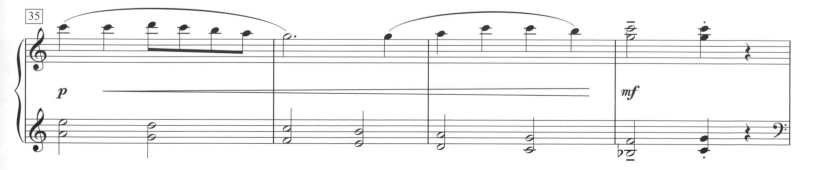

13

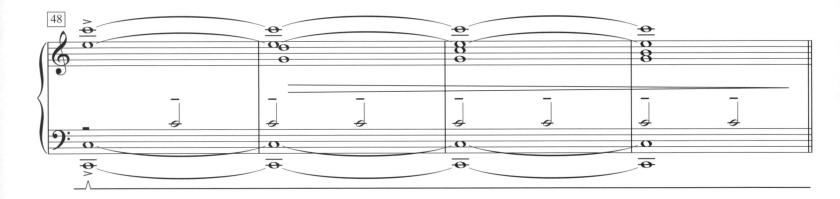

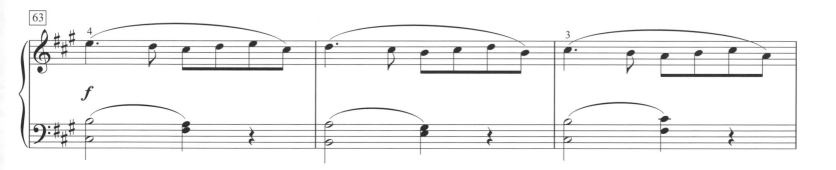

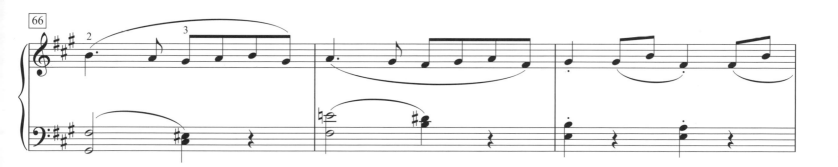

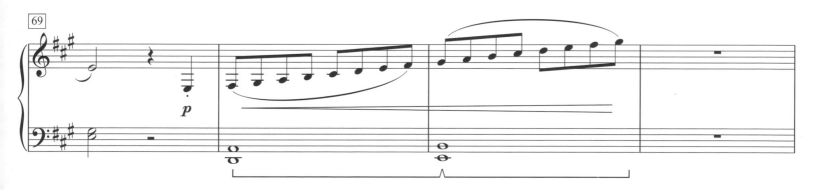

GOD REST YE MERRY, GENTLEMEN

Traditional English Carol
Arranged by Phillip Keveren

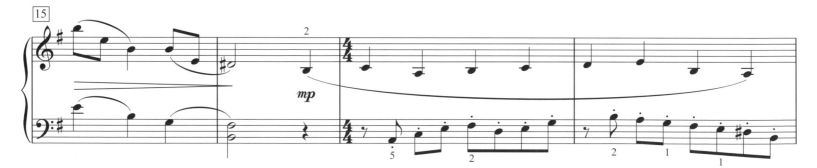

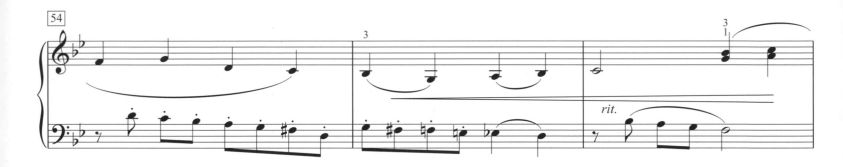

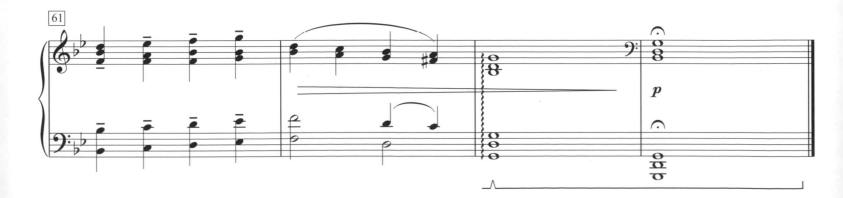

THE HURON CAROL
('Twas in the Moon of Wintertime)

Traditional French-Canadian Text
Traditional Canadian-Indian Melody
Arranged by Phillip Keveren

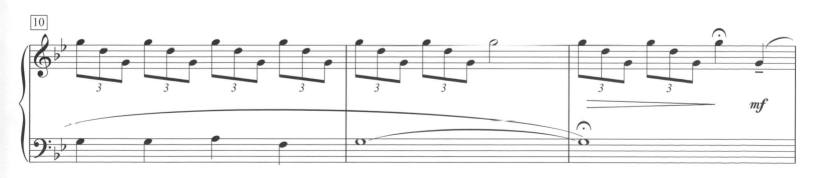

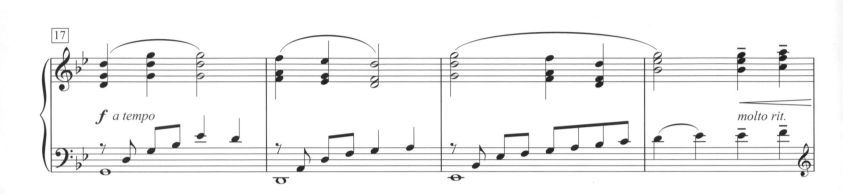

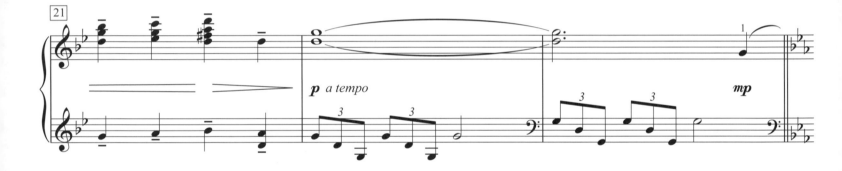

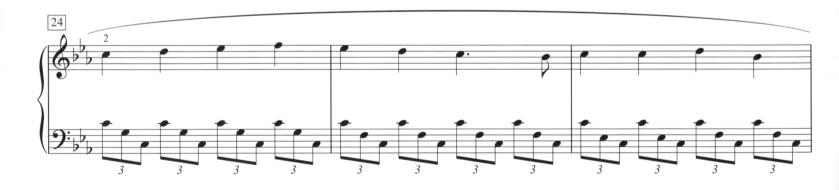

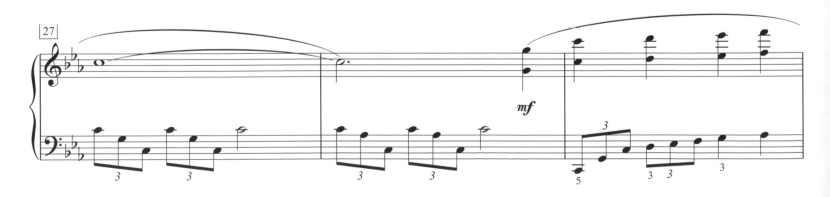

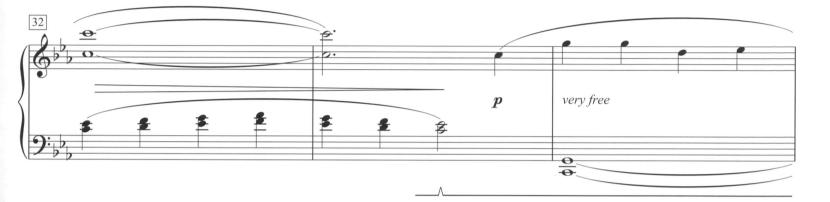

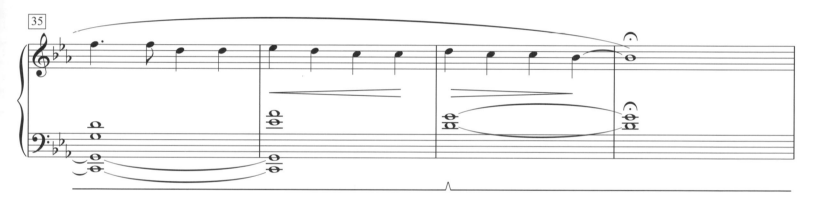

IN THE BLEAK MIDWINTER

Poem by CHRISTINA ROSSETTI
Music by GUSTAV HOLST
Arranged by Phillip Keveren

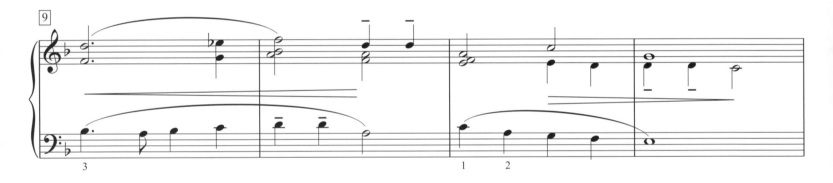

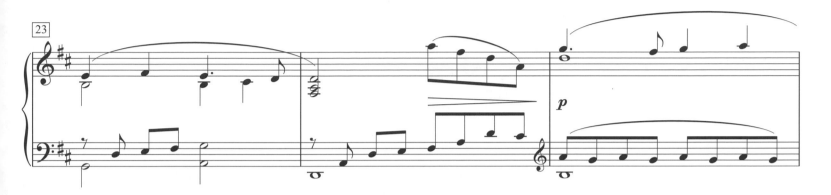

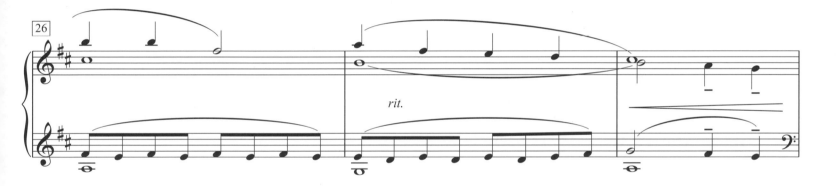

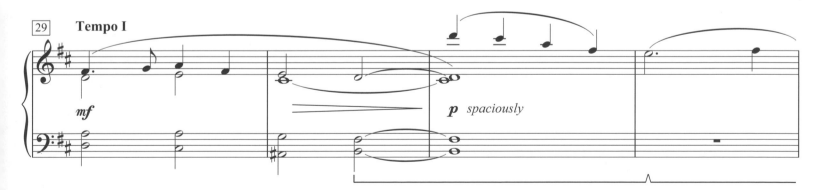

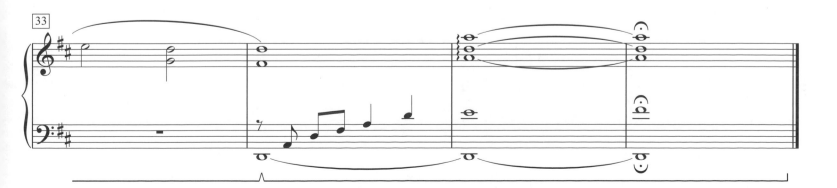

IT CAME UPON THE MIDNIGHT CLEAR

Words by EDMUND HAMILTON SEARS
Music by RICHARD STORRS WILLIS
Arranged by Phillip Keveren

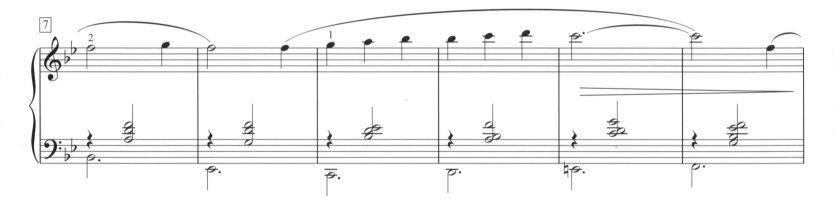

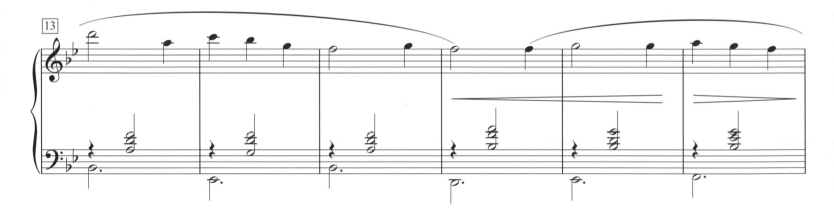

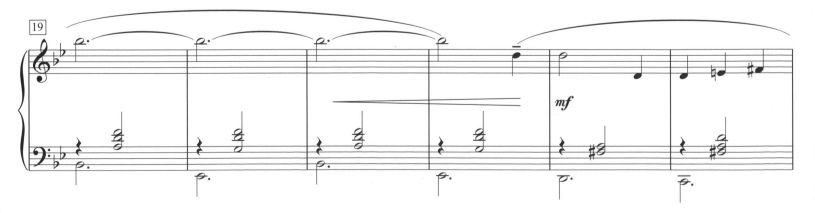

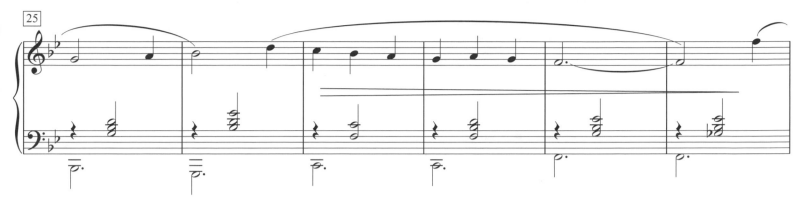

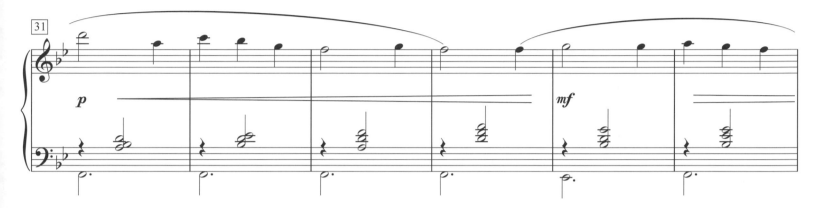

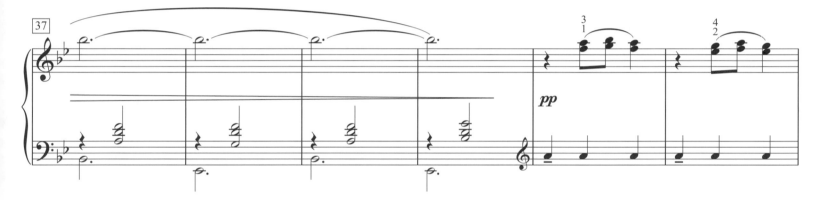

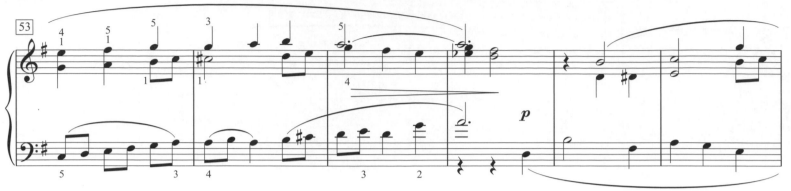

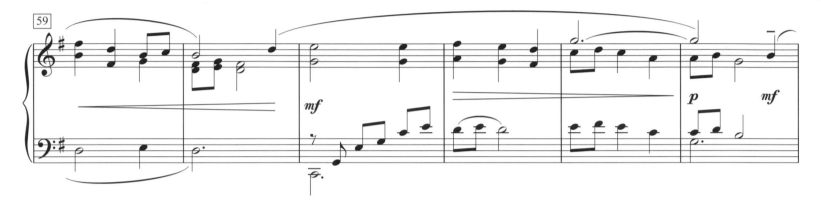

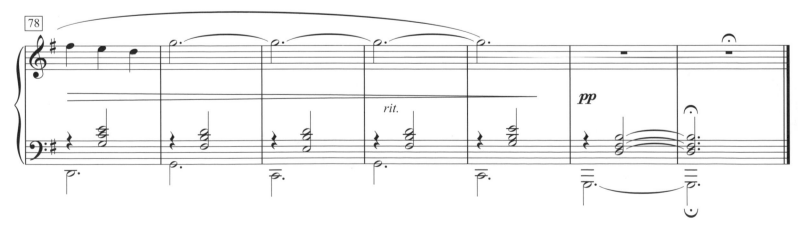

JOY TO THE WORLD

Words by ISAAC WATTS
Music by GEORGE FRIDERIC HANDEL
Adapted by LOWELL MASON
Arranged by Phillip Keveren

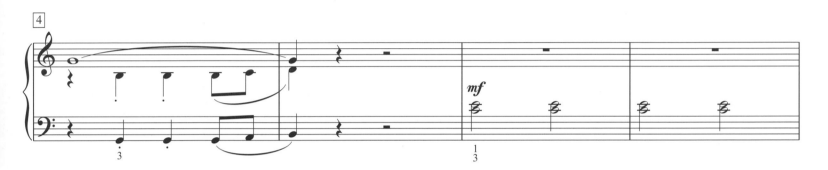

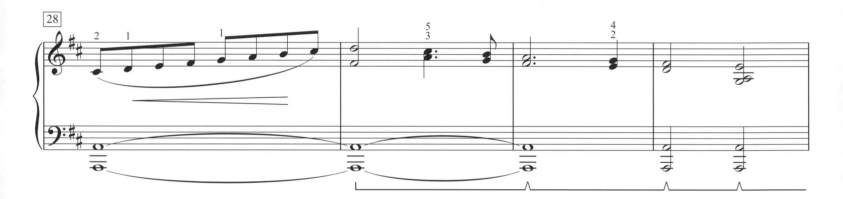

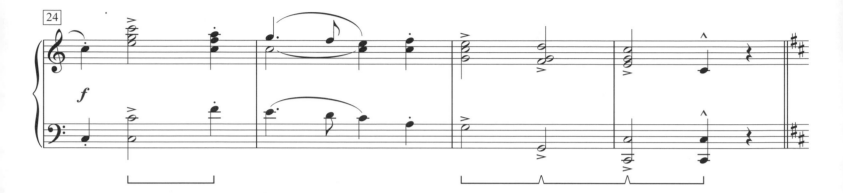

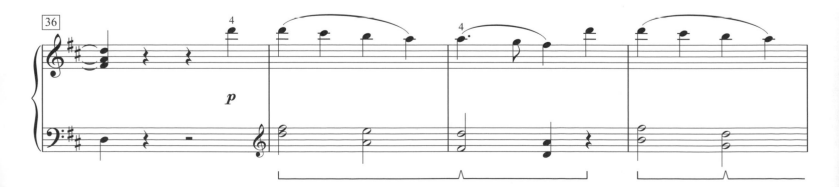

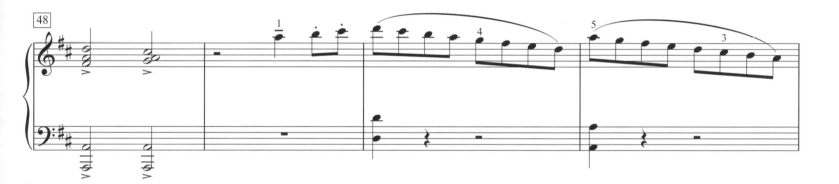

LET ALL MORTAL FLESH KEEP SILENCE

Words from the Liturgy of St. James
Translated by GERARD MOULTRIE
17th Century French Carol
Arranged by Phillip Keveren

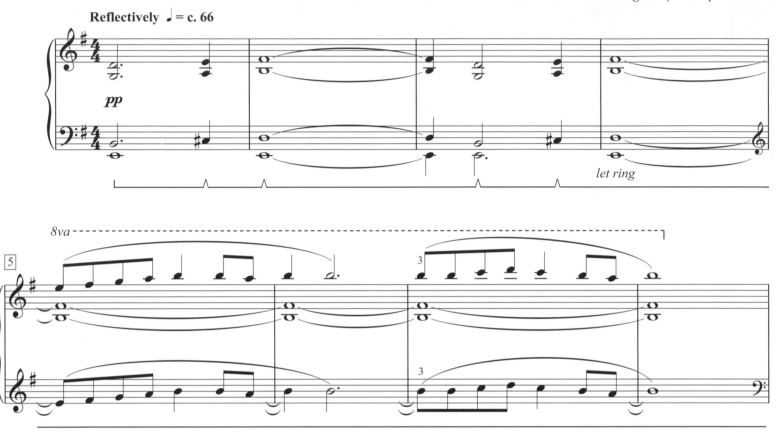

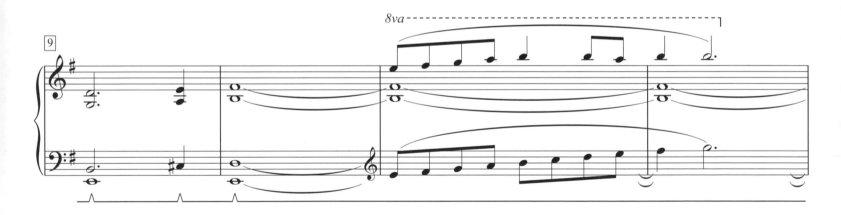

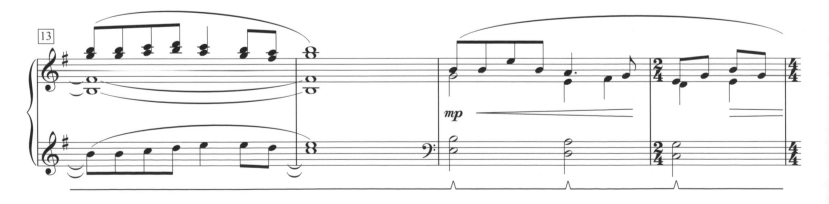

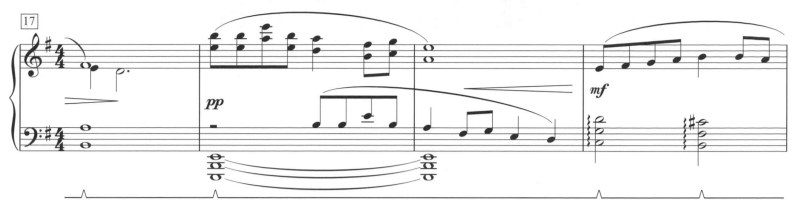

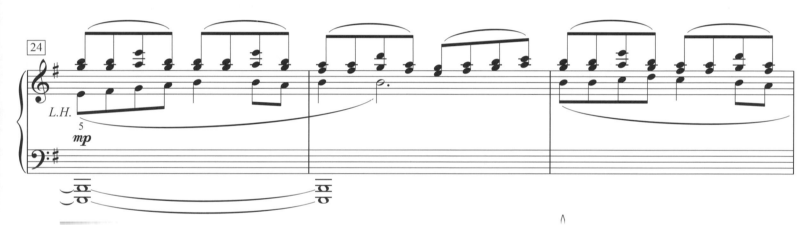

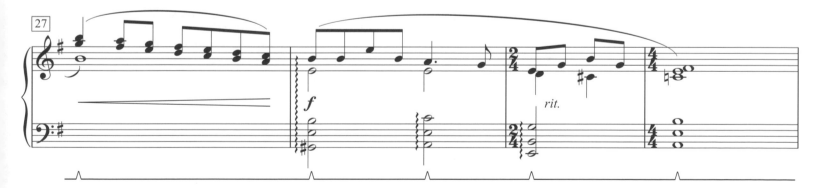

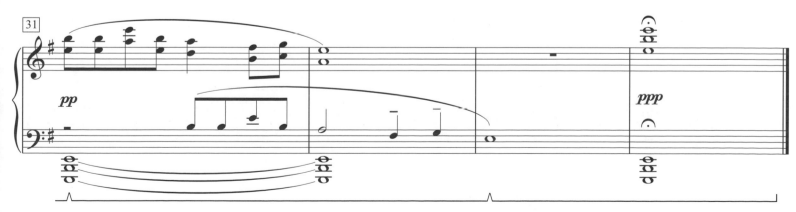

O COME, ALL YE FAITHFUL

Music by JOHN FRANCIS WADE
Latin Words translated by FREDERICK OAKELEY
Arranged by Phillip Keveren

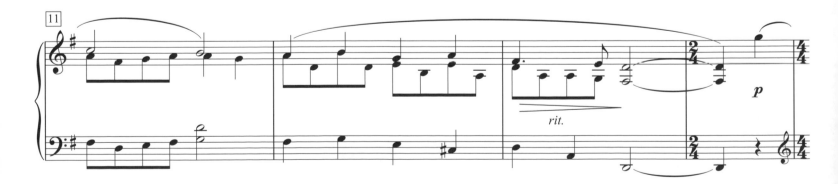

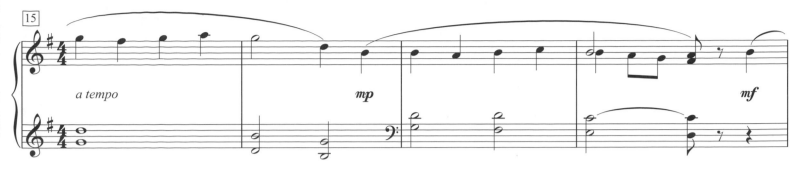

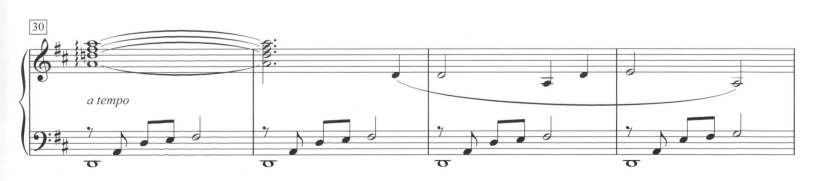

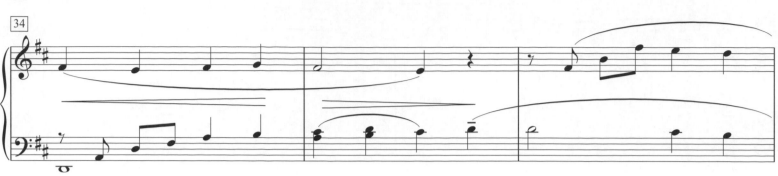

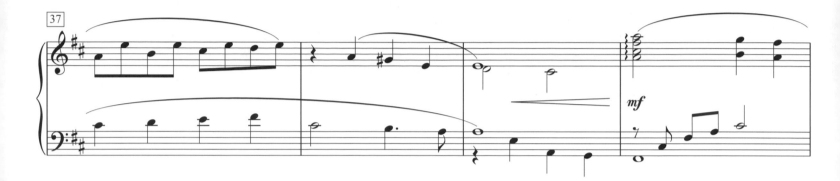

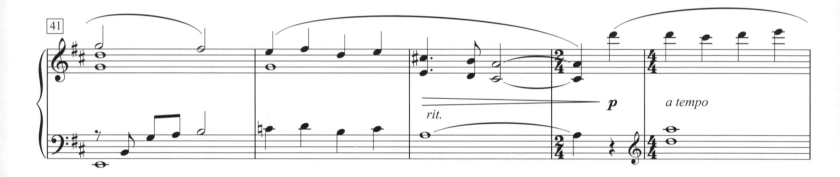

SILENT NIGHT

Words by JOSEPH MOHR
Translated by JOHN F. YOUNG
Music by FRANZ X. GRUBER
Arranged by Phillip Keveren

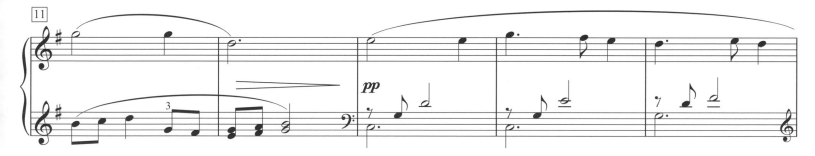

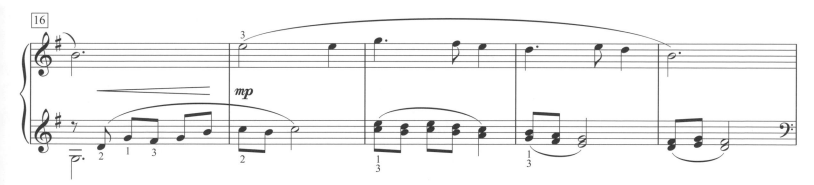

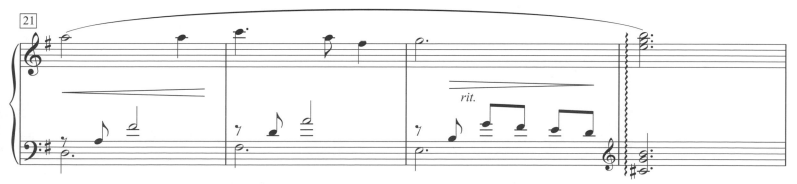

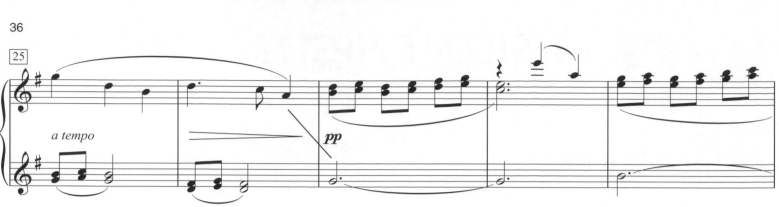

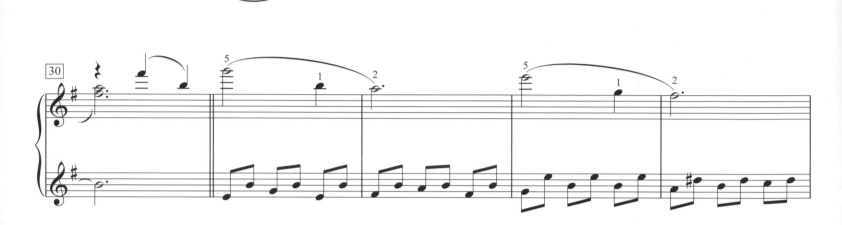

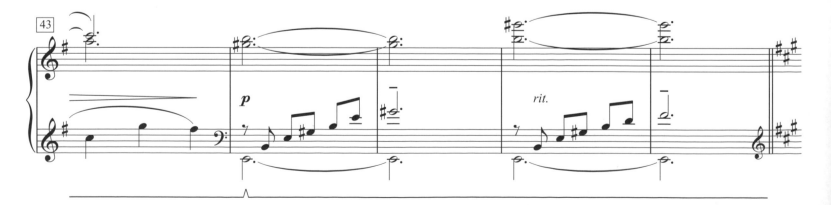

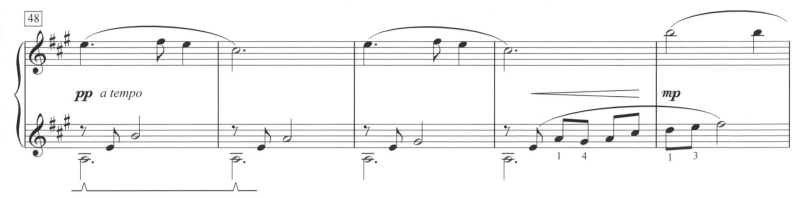

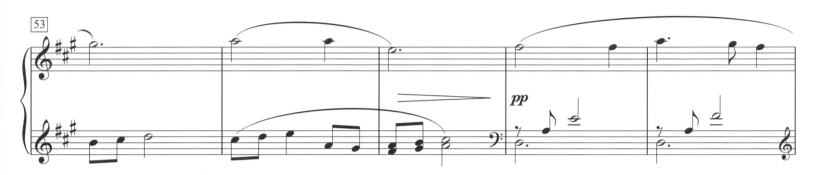

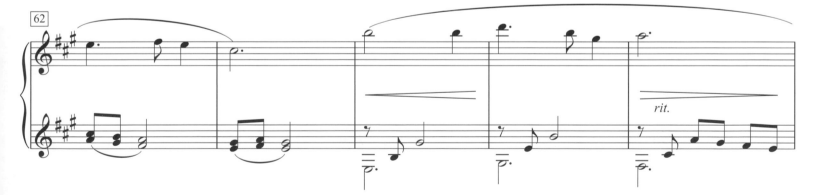

O HOLY NIGHT

French Words by PLACIDE CAPPEAU
English Words by JOHN S. DWIGHT
Music by ADOLPHE ADAM
Arranged by Phillip Keveren

Reverently, with rubato ♩. = 60

p legato

With pedal

poco rit.   *a tempo*

STILL, STILL, STILL

Salzburg Melody, c. 1819
Traditional Austrian Text
Arranged by Phillip Keveren

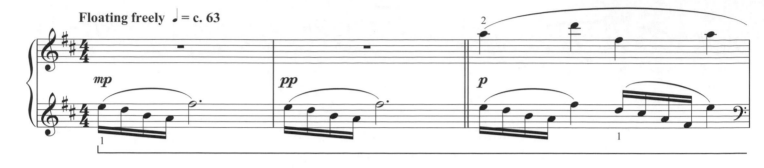

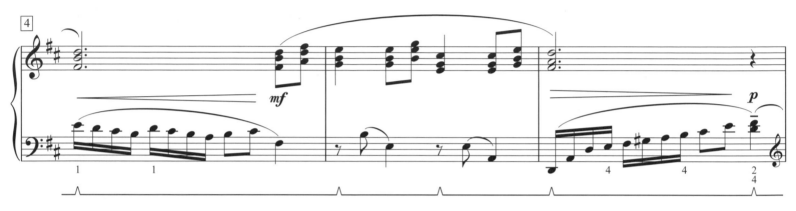

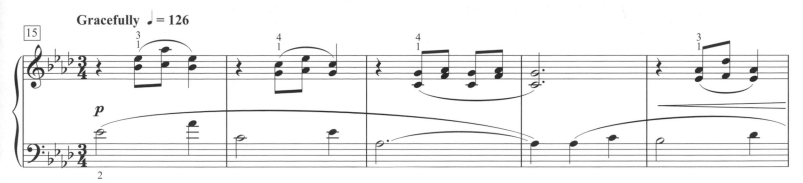

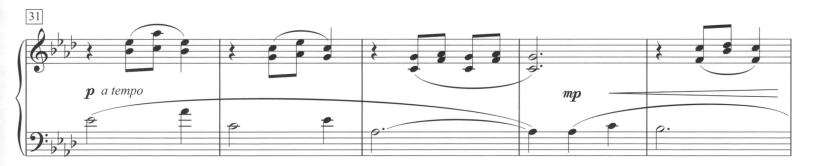

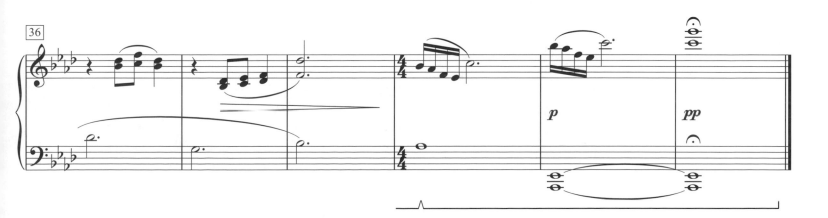

WE THREE KINGS OF ORIENT ARE

Words and Music by
JOHN H. HOPKINS, JR.
Arranged by Phillip Keveren

Flowing ♩ = c. 126

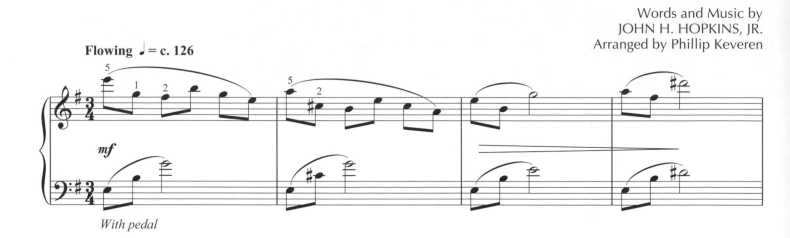

With pedal

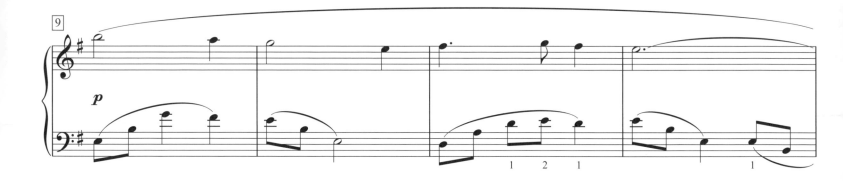

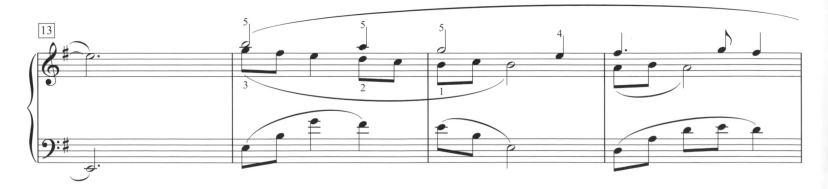

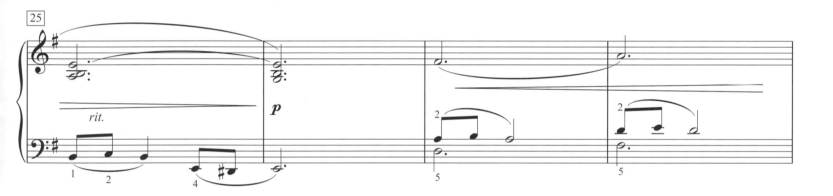

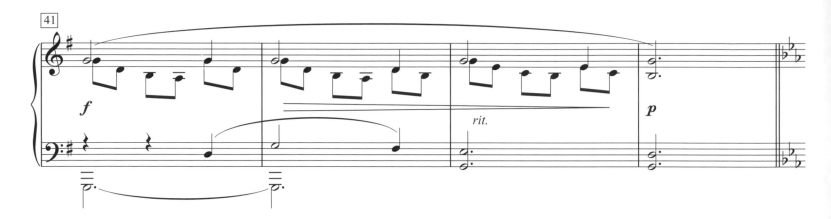

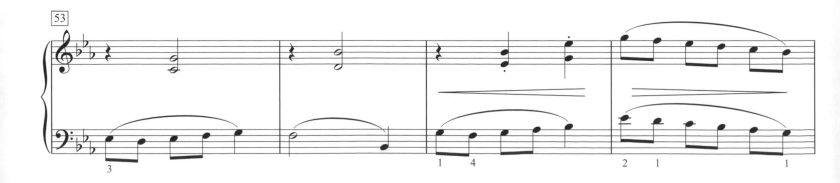

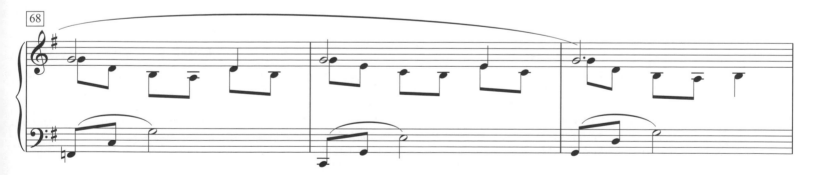

THE PHILLIP KEVEREN SERIES

PIANO SOLO

00156644	**ABBA for Classical Piano**	$15.99
00311024	**Above All**	$12.99
00311348	**Americana**	$12.99
00198473	**Bach Meets Jazz**	$14.99
00313594	**Bacharach and David**	$15.99
00306412	**The Beatles**	$17.99
00312189	**The Beatles for Classical Piano**	$16.99
00275876	**The Beatles – Recital Suites**	$19.99
00312546	**Best Piano Solos**	$15.99
00156601	**Blessings**	$12.99
00198656	**Blues Classics**	$12.99
00284359	**Broadway Songs with a Classical Flair**	$14.99
00310669	**Broadway's Best**	$14.99
00312106	**Canzone Italiana**	$12.99
00280848	**Carpenters**	$16.99
00310629	**A Celtic Christmas**	$12.99
00310549	**The Celtic Collection**	$12.95
00280571	**Celtic Songs with a Classical Flair**	$12.99
00263362	**Charlie Brown Favorites**	$14.99
00312190	**Christmas at the Movies**	$14.99
00294754	**Christmas Carols with a Classical Flair**	$12.99
00311414	**Christmas Medleys**	$14.99
00236669	**Christmas Praise Hymns**	$12.99
00233788	**Christmas Songs for Classical Piano**	$12.99
00311769	**Christmas Worship Medleys**	$14.99
00310607	**Cinema Classics**	$15.99
00301857	**Circles**	$10.99
00311101	**Classic Wedding Songs**	$10.95
00311292	**Classical Folk**	$10.95
00311083	**Classical Jazz**	$12.95
00137779	**Coldplay for Classical Piano**	$16.99
00311103	**Contemporary Wedding Songs**	$12.99
00348788	**Country Songs with a Classical Flair**	$14.99
00249097	**Disney Recital Suites**	$17.99
00311754	**Disney Songs for Classical Piano**	$17.99
00241379	**Disney Songs for Ragtime Piano**	$17.99
00311881	**Favorite Wedding Songs**	$14.99
00315974	**Fiddlin' at the Piano**	$12.99
00311811	**The Film Score Collection**	$15.99
00269408	**Folksongs with a Classical Flair**	$12.99
00144353	**The Gershwin Collection**	$14.99
00233789	**Golden Scores**	$14.99
00144351	**Gospel Greats**	$12.99
00183566	**The Great American Songbook**	$12.99
00312084	**The Great Melodies**	$12.99
00311157	**Great Standards**	$12.95
00171621	**A Grown-Up Christmas List**	$12.99
00311071	**The Hymn Collection**	$12.99
00311349	**Hymn Medleys**	$12.99

00280705	**Hymns in a Celtic Style**	$12.99
00269407	**Hymns with a Classical Flair**	$12.99
00311249	**Hymns with a Touch of Jazz**	$12.99
00310905	**I Could Sing of Your Love Forever**	$12.95
00310762	**Jingle Jazz**	$14.99
00175310	**Billy Joel for Classical Piano**	$16.99
00126449	**Elton John for Classical Piano**	$16.99
00310839	**Let Freedom Ring!**	$12.99
00238988	**Andrew Lloyd Webber Piano Songbook**	$14.99
00313227	**Andrew Lloyd Webber Solos**	$15.99
00313523	**Mancini Magic**	$16.99
00312113	**More Disney Songs for Classical Piano**	$16.99
00311295	**Motown Hits**	$14.99
00300640	**Piano Calm**	$12.99
00339131	**Piano Calm: Christmas**	$12.99
00346009	**Piano Calm: Prayer**	$14.99
00306870	**Piazzolla Tangos**	$16.99
00156645	**Queen for Classical Piano**	$15.99
00310755	**Richard Rodgers Classics**	$16.99
00289545	**Scottish Songs**	$12.99
00310609	**Shout to the Lord!**	$14.99
00119403	**The Sound of Music**	$14.99
00311978	**The Spirituals Collection**	$10.99
00210445	**Star Wars**	$16.99
00224738	**Symphonic Hymns for Piano**	$14.99
00279673	**Tin Pan Alley**	$12.99
00312112	**Treasured Hymns for Classical Piano**	$14.99
00144926	**The Twelve Keys of Christmas**	$12.99
00278486	**The Who for Classical Piano**	$16.99
00294036	**Worship with a Touch of Jazz**	$12.99
00311911	**Yuletide Jazz**	$17.99

EASY PIANO

00210401	**Adele for Easy Classical Piano**	$15.99
00310610	**African-American Spirituals**	$10.99
00218244	**The Beatles for Easy Classical Piano**	$14.99
00218387	**Catchy Songs for Piano**	$12.99
00310973	**Celtic Dreams**	$12.99
00233686	**Christmas Carols for Easy Classical Piano**	$12.99
00311126	**Christmas Pops**	$14.99
00311548	**Classic Pop/Rock Hits**	$14.99
00310769	**A Classical Christmas**	$10.95
00310975	**Classical Movie Themes**	$12.99
00144352	**Disney Songs for Easy Classical Piano**	$12.99
00311093	**Early Rock 'n' Roll**	$14.99
00311997	**Easy Worship Medleys**	$12.99
00289547	**Duke Ellington**	$14.99
00160297	**Folksongs for Easy Classical Piano**	$12.99

00110374	**George Gershwin Classics**	$12.99
00310805	**Gospel Treasures**	$12.99
00306821	**Vince Guaraldi Collection**	$19.99
00160294	**Hymns for Easy Classical Piano**	$12.99
00310798	**Immortal Hymns**	$12.99
00311294	**Jazz Standards**	$12.99
00310744	**Love Songs**	$12.99
00233740	**The Most Beautiful Songs for Easy Classical Piano**	$12.99
00220036	**Pop Ballads**	$14.99
00311406	**Pop Gems of the 1950s**	$12.95
00311407	**Pop Gems of the 1960s**	$12.95
00233739	**Pop Standards for Easy Classical Piano**	$12.99
00102887	**A Ragtime Christmas**	$12.99
00311293	**Ragtime Classics**	$10.95
00312028	**Santa Swings**	$12.99
00233688	**Songs from Childhood for Easy Classical Piano**	$12.99
00103258	**Songs of Inspiration**	$12.99
00310840	**Sweet Land of Liberty**	$12.99
00126450	**10,000 Reasons**	$14.99
00310712	**Timeless Praise**	$12.95
00311086	**TV Themes**	$12.99
00310717	**21 Great Classics**	$12.99
00160076	**Waltzes & Polkas for Easy Classical Piano**	$12.99
00145342	**Weekly Worship**	$16.99

BIG-NOTE PIANO

00310838	**Children's Favorite Movie Songs**	$12.99
00346000	**Christmas Movie Magic**	$12.99
00277368	**Classical Favorites**	$12.99
00310907	**Contemporary Hits**	$12.99
00277370	**Disney Favorites**	$14.99
00310888	**Joy to the World**	$12.99
00310908	**The Nutcracker**	$12.99
00277371	**Star Wars**	$16.99

BEGINNING PIANO SOLOS

00311202	**Awesome God**	$12.99
00310837	**Christian Children's Favorites**	$12.99
00311117	**Christmas Traditions**	$10.99
00311250	**Easy Hymns**	$12.99
00102710	**Everlasting God**	$10.99
00311403	**Jazzy Tunes**	$10.95
00310822	**Kids' Favorites**	$12.99
00338175	**Silly Songs for Kids**	$9.99

PIANO DUET

00126452	**The Christmas Variations**	$12.99
00311350	**Classical Theme Duets**	$10.99
00295099	**Gospel Duets**	$12.99
00311544	**Hymn Duets**	$14.99
00311203	**Praise & Worship Duets**	$12.99
00294755	**Sacred Christmas Duets**	$12.99
00119405	**Star Wars**	$14.99
00253545	**Worship Songs for Two**	$12.99